HOT! BRIGHT QUILTING™

HOUSE of
WHITE
BIRCHES

PUBLISHERS
SINCE 1947

Introduction

There are so many bright-colored prints available to quilters today. Everywhere you look in both the fashion and decorating world, the colors are hot and lively. Instead of earth tones and somber dark colors, bright colors abound.

Each project included in this book uses lots of different fabrics to create a scrappy look. You may use scraps, but if your scrap basket doesn't include lots of bright prints, purchase a variety of fat quarters. These will give you a wide range of prints without investing lots of money. Fat quarters make it easy to broaden your fabric horizons to include lots of colors.

If you want to liven up your quilting with some colorful projects, get ready for some fun making *Hot Bright Quilting*. ■

Meet the Designer
Kate Laucomer

I made my first quilt with my grandma when I was 12, my second quilt in about 1978, and then I didn't quilt again until 1988. It was then that I became addicted.

Rod and I have been married almost 27 years and we have three kids. Our oldest son Chad married Larissa this last year, so now I'm a mother-in-law. Sam is in high school and Kali is in middle school! I homeschool the kids, so our days are very full (algebra … what fun!) and quilting time is very precious to me.

In my "spare" time, I do quilt. In 1993, I started my pattern company Homespun Charm (a legitimate reason to buy more fabric!). I like mostly country-looking patterns with blanket-stitched appliqué. They're kind of primitive but don't

have the cookie-cutter look. I love plaids and stars and have made several giant star plaid quilts that have a lot of machine-quilted feathers on them. I'm also active in our local guild, our workshop and our state guild.

So, what am I doing with a book on hot, bright quilts, you might be asking yourself. The minute Kali learned to crawl, she would get her hot, bright quilt my girlfriend made her and completely ignore the more country-looking quilt I had made. From that time on, bright fabrics have slowly crept into my stash. Besides, I live in Nebraska. Those bright fabrics are mighty appealing during our long, dull, gray winters.

I hope you enjoy the book.

Table of Contents

Fractured Stars

Bright yellow and orange pieces create the blades in this unusual star design.

PROJECT SPECIFICATIONS
Skill Level: Intermediate
Quilt Size: 40" x 40"
Block Size: 10" x 10"
Number of Blocks: 16

FABRIC & BATTING
- 1¼ yards medium orange mottled
- 1¼ yards bright yellow dot
- 2¼ yards dark orange tonal
- Backing 46" x 46"
- Batting 46" x 46"

SUPPLIES & TOOLS
- Neutral color all-purpose thread
- Quilting thread
- Basic sewing tools and supplies

Cutting
1. Make 65 copies of the paper-piecing pattern given.

2. Cut four 2¼" by fabric width strips dark orange tonal for binding.

Completing the Blocks
1. Cut apart one copy of the paper-piecing pattern on the solid lines as shown in Figure 1.

Figure 1   **Figure 2**

2. Use each piece to rough-cut a fabric piece as shown in Figure 2, placing the pattern on the wrong side of the fabric and cutting the pieces at

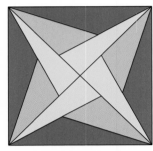

Fractured Star
10" x 10" Block

least ¼" larger all around than the paper piece to allow for seam allowance and to allow a bit of leeway in arranging the pieces before stitching.

3. Place fabric to cover area 1 on another paper pattern with wrong side of fabric against the unmarked side of the paper, allowing fabric to extend at least ¼" into adjacent areas as shown in Figure 3.

Figure 3   **Figure 4**

4. Place fabric for area 2 right sides together with fabric 1 on the 1-2 edge as shown in Figure 4; pin along the 1-2 line. Fold fabric 2 over to cover area 2, allowing fabric to extend at least ¼" into adjacent areas as shown in Figure 5. Adjust fabric if necessary. Unfold fabric 2; pin to lie flat on piece 1.

Figure 5

5. Flip paper pattern; stitch on the 1-2 line, beginning and ending 2 or 3 stitches into adjacent areas as shown in Figure 6. Stitch to (or beyond) the outside heavy solid line on outer areas as shown in Figure 7.

Figure 6   **Figure 7**

6. Trim the 1-2 seam allowance to $1/8$"–$1/4$" as shown in Figure 8. Fold fabric 2 to cover area 2; lightly press with a warm dry iron.

Figure 8   **Figure 9**

7. Continue to add fabrics in numerical order to cover the paper pattern as shown in Figure 9. Check that each piece will cover its area before stitching. **Note:** *The very short stitches are hard to remove and often cause a tear in the paper pattern. Should this happen, place a small piece of transparent tape over the tear to continue to use the pattern. Do not use this quick fix frequently, as it makes removal of the paper difficult.*

8. Trim paper and fabric edges even on the outside heavy solid line as shown in Figure 10.

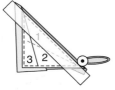

Figure 10

9. Complete 64 paper-pieced sections.

10. Place two block sections fabric sides together. Stick a pin through both sections at each end

of the dashed seam line to be sure the lines on both sections match as shown in Figure 11. Stitch along the dashed seam lines to join the sections as shown in Figure 12. Remove paper from seam-allowance area only; press seam to one side.

Figure 11   **Figure 12**

11. Join two more sections; press. Join the two joined sections to complete one block referring to the block drawing; press seams to one side. Repeat for 16 blocks. **Note:** *Leave paper pattern intact until the blocks are joined.*

Completing the Top

1. Join four blocks to make a row as shown in Figure 13; repeat for four rows. Press seams in adjoining rows in opposite directions.

Figure 13

2. Join the rows to complete the pieced top; press seams in one direction.

3. Remove all paper pieces.

Completing the Quilt

1. Sandwich the batting between the completed top and prepared backing; pin or baste layers together to hold.

2. Quilt as desired by hand or machine; remove pins or basting. Trim excess backing and batting even with quilt top.

3. Join binding strips on short ends to make one long strip. Fold the strip in half along length with wrong sides together; press.

4. Sew binding to quilt edges, mitering corners and overlapping ends. Fold binding to the back side and stitch in place to finish. ■

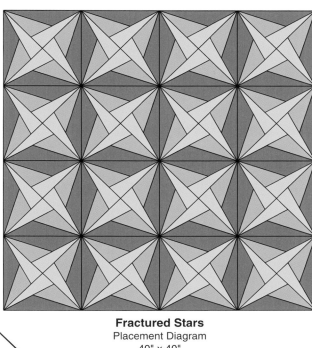

Fractured Stars
Placement Diagram
40" x 40"

① dark orange

③ yellow

② medium orange

Paper-Piecing Pattern
Make 65 copies

Round & Round We Go

Mix up your bright prints in the simple Around the Square design.

PROJECT NOTES

The instructions given here will result in a twin-size quilt. Vary the number of blocks to create different-size projects as shown with the accompanying drawings.

PROJECT SPECIFICATIONS

Skill Level: Beginner
Quilt Size: 70" x 90"
Block Size: 10" x 10"
Number of Blocks: 63

FABRIC & BATTING

- Assorted bright prints or fat quarters to total 6 yards
- 5/8 yard orange print for binding
- Backing 76" x 96"
- Batting 76" x 96"

SUPPLIES & TOOLS

- Neutral color all-purpose thread
- Quilting thread
- Basic sewing tools and supplies

Cutting

1. Cut (63) 4^1/$_2$" x 4^1/$_2$" A squares from assorted bright prints.

2. Cut (252) 3^1/$_2$" x 7^1/$_2$" B rectangles from assorted bright prints.

3. Cut eight 2^1/$_4$" by fabric width strips orange print for binding.

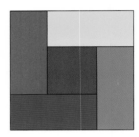

Around the Square
10" x 10" Block

Completing the Blocks

1. Select one A and four B pieces. **Note:** *Do not use the same fabric twice in one block.*

2. To complete one block, place one B rectangle right sides together with the A square. Starting at the matching A-B edge, sew a ^{1}/$_4$" seam 2" down the unit to make a partial seam as shown in Figure 1.

Figure 1

3. Press the stitched part of the seam of the A-B unit toward B.

4. Sew a second B rectangle to the stitched end of the A-B unit as shown in Figure 2; press seam toward B.

Figure 2

5. Repeat with a third and fourth B rectangle; press seams toward B.

6. Complete the partial seam to complete one block as shown in Figure 3; press seam toward B. Repeat for 63 blocks.

Figure 3

Completing the Top

1. Arrange the completed blocks in nine rows of seven blocks each referring to the Placement Diagram.

2. Join the blocks in rows as arranged; press seams in adjacent rows in opposite directions.

3. Join the rows as arranged to complete the pieced top; press seams in one direction.

Completing the Quilt

1. Sandwich the batting between the completed top and prepared backing; pin or baste layers together to hold.

2. Quilt as desired by hand or machine; remove pins or basting. Trim excess backing and batting even with quilt top.

3. Join binding strips on short ends to make one long strip. Fold the strip in half along length with wrong sides together; press.

4. Sew binding to quilt edges, mitering corners and overlapping ends. Fold binding to the back side and stitch in place to finish. ■

Round & Round We Go
Placement Diagram
70" x 90"

Cutting Fat Quarters

To make the best use of fat quarters, Figure 4 shows two possible cutting configurations.

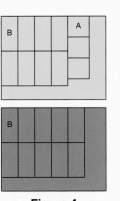

Figure 4

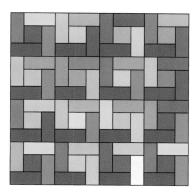

Round & Round We Go Table Topper
Placement Diagram
40" x 40"
16 Blocks
4 rows of 4 blocks each

Round & Round We Go Throw
Placement Diagram
60" x 60"
36 Blocks
6 rows of 6 blocks each

Round & Round We Go Queen Quilt
Placement Diagram
90" x 90"
81 Blocks
9 rows of 9 blocks each

Cheese & Crackers

Ragged circles on a triangle/square background create colorful movement in this neat lap-size quilt.

PROJECT NOTES

The instructions given here will result in a lap-size quilt. Vary the number and placement of the blocks to create smaller or larger quilts with a whole new look.

PROJECT SPECIFICATIONS

Skill Level: Beginner
Quilt Size: 60" x 60"
Block Size: 10" x 10"
Number of Blocks: 36

FABRIC & BATTING

- 18 (^{1}/$_2$-yard pieces) or 36 fat quarters assorted bright prints
- Backing 66" x 66"
- Batting 66" x 66"

SUPPLIES & TOOLS

- Bright color or variegated all-purpose thread
- Quilting thread
- Template plastic
- 12" or 12^1/$_2$" acrylic square
- Washable fabric marker
- Basic sewing tools and supplies

Cutting

1. Trace A and B patterns onto template plastic and label. *Note: The circles are not really circles. They were made from circles that have been cut in half and had seam allowances added to the center. Cut as directed on each piece.*

2. Make plastic templates for Circles 1 and 2 using patterns given.

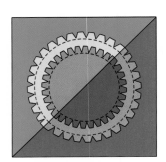

Cheese & Crackers
10" x 10" Block

3. Cut (36) 11^1/$_2$" x 11^1/$_2$" C squares assorted bright prints.

4. Cut 2^1/$_4$"-wide bias strips from assorted bright prints and join with diagonal seams to make a 250" length for binding.

Completing the Blocks

1. Using the A and B templates as guides, press each fabric A and B piece in half vertically and horizontally on the centerlines as shown in Figure 1.

Figure 1

2. Press each C square in half on both diagonals to create crease lines to mark the centers.

3. Place the Circle 1 template on the right side of one A fabric circle, matching line on template with pressed lines on the fabric circle.

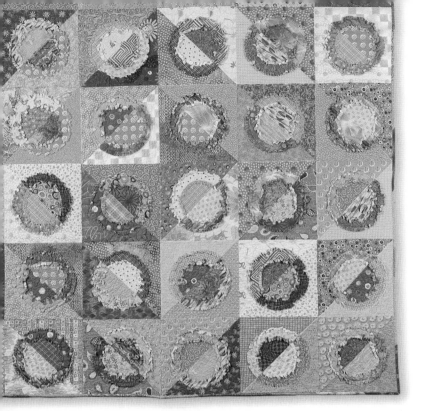

9. Cut each stitched unit in half on the main pressed centerline to make half blocks as shown in Figure 4.

Figure 4

Figure 5

10. Turn each half block over so the wrong side is up; very carefully trim the background C fabric away from behind the A/B half circle leaving a 1/4" seam allowance as shown in Figure 5.

11. Select two half blocks and join on the diagonal to complete one Cheese & Crackers block as shown in Figure 6; press seam open. Repeat for 36 blocks.

Figure 6

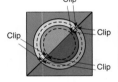

Figure 7

12. Carefully clip the loose raw edges of each circle at both sides of the diagonal seam as close to the seam as possible as shown in Figure 7.

13. Using a long basting thread, fold the raw edge of the A circle over the stitching and baste in place as shown in Figure 8. **Note:** *This step is optional, but keeps the loose edge out of way when quilting.*

Figure 8

Figure 9

14. Trim each block to 10$\frac{1}{2}$" x 10$\frac{1}{2}$" using the acrylic ruler, keeping the A and B circles centered as shown in Figure 9.

4. Trace around the template with the washable fabric marker; repeat on each A and B fabric circle.

5. Lay out all of the C squares on a flat surface; place one A circle and one B circle with each square. **Note:** *Try to avoid having two blocks with the same fabric combinations.*

6. Position one square right side up with the chosen A fabric circle right side up on top using pressed lines to align centers.

7. Center and pin a B fabric circle right side up on the layered A-C unit using pressed lines as guides for centering. **Note:** *Be sure the A and B circles are aligned so the shapes match as shown in Figure 2.* Repeat for 36 units.

Figure 2

Figure 3

8. Stitch on each marked line as shown in Figure 3. Repeat for all pinned units.

 HOUSE OF WHITE BIRCHES, BERNE, INDIANA 46711   WWW.WHITEBIRCHES.COM

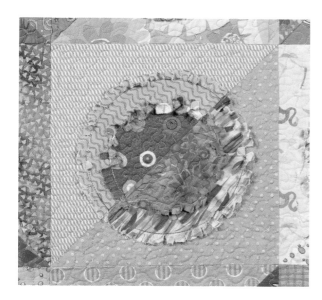

Completing the Top

1. Join six blocks to make a row as shown in Figure 10; press seams in one direction. Repeat for six rows. **Note:** *You may change the positioning of the blocks as is shown in the alternate Placement Diagrams given.*

Figure 10

2. Join the rows referring to the Placement Diagram to complete the pieced center. Press seams in one direction.

Completing the Quilt

1. Sandwich the batting between the completed top and prepared backing; pin or baste layers together to hold.

2. Quilt in the block backgrounds and in the center of the B circle areas as desired by hand or machine; remove pins or basting. Trim excess backing and batting even with quilt top.

3. Fold the bias binding strip in half along length with wrong sides together; press.

4. Sew binding to quilt edges, mitering corners and overlapping ends. Fold binding to the back side and stitch in place.

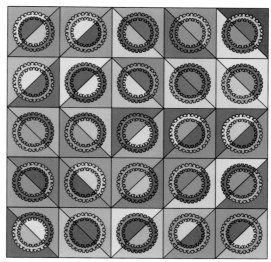

Cheese & Crackers
Placement Diagram
50" x 50"
Asymmetrical Arrangement

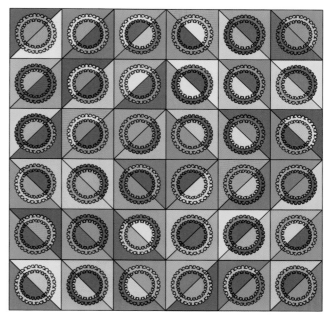

Cheese & Crackers
Placement Diagram
60" x 60"

5. Remove basting on circles. Clip just to the stitching lines every $3/16$" on edges of all circle pieces.

6. Wash the quilt on your washer's longest setting; dry on normal. Wash again, if necessary, to make a more ragged look. ■

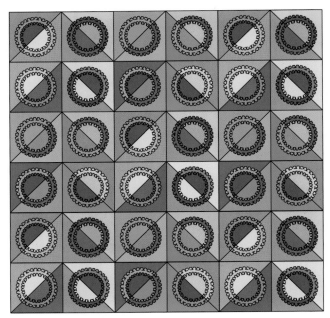

Cheese & Crackers
Placement Diagram
60" x 60"
Alternative Layout

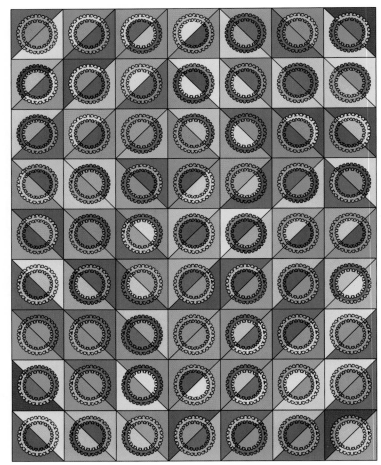

Cheese & Crackers Twin Quilt
Placement Diagram
70" x 90"
63 Blocks

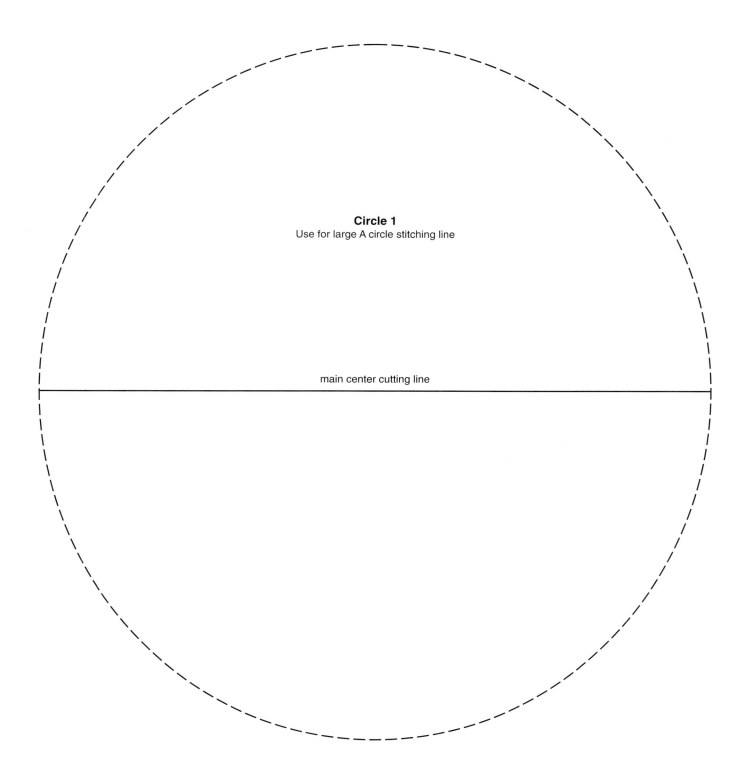

Circle 1
Use for large A circle stitching line

main center cutting line

A
Cut 36 assorted bright prints

main center cutting line

HOUSE OF WHITE BIRCHES, BERNE, INDIANA 46711   WWW.WHITEBIRCHES.COM

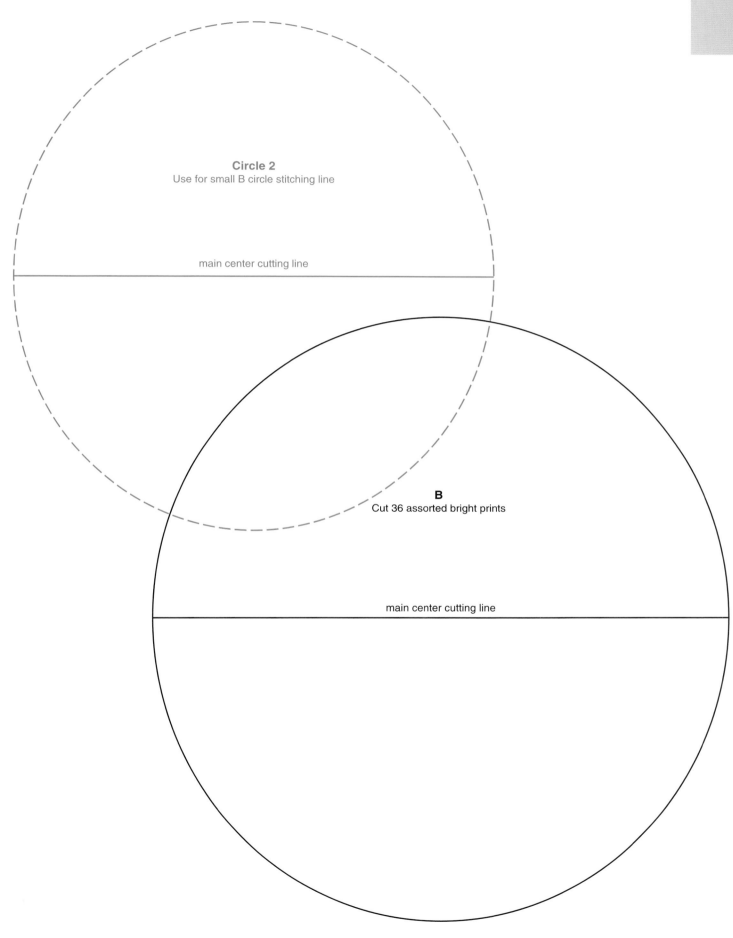

Circle 2
Use for small B circle stitching line

main center cutting line

B
Cut 36 assorted bright prints

main center cutting line

Crooked Paths

Crooked paths are created in a zigzag pattern across the top of this bed-size quilt.

PROJECT NOTES

The instructions given here will result in a twin-size quilt. Vary the number of blocks per row and the number of rows to create different-size projects as shown with the accompanying drawings.

PROJECT SPECIFICATIONS

Skill Level: Beginner
Quilt Size: 70" x 90"
Block Size: 10" x 10"
Number of Blocks: 48

FABRIC & BATTING

- 1/2 yard each 8 different bright prints
- 1 7/8 yards multicolor print
- 2 1/2 yards lime green print
- Backing 76" x 96"
- Batting 76" x 96"

SUPPLIES & TOOLS

- Neutral color all-purpose thread
- Quilting thread
- Basic sewing tools and supplies

Cutting

1. Cut (14) 5 7/8" by fabric width strips lime green print; subcut strips into (96) 5 7/8" A squares.

2. Cut two 5 7/8" by fabric width strips from each of the eight bright prints; subcut strips into (12) 5 7/8" B squares of each fabric.

3. Cut eight 5 1/2" by fabric width strips multicolor print. Join strips on short ends to make one long strip; press seams open. Subcut strip into two 80 1/2" C strips and two 70 1/2" D strips.

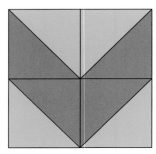

Zigzag
10" x 10" Block

4. Cut eight 2 1/4" by fabric width strips multicolor print for binding.

Completing the Blocks

1. Draw a diagonal line from corner to corner on the wrong side of each A square.

2. Layer an A square with a B square with right sides together.

3. Stitch 1/4" on each side of the marked line on the layered units as shown in Figure 1.

Figure 1

4. Cut apart on the marked line and press B open to complete two A-B units as shown in Figure 2; repeat for 192 units.

Figure 2   **Figure 3**

5. Select four same-color A-B units; join two units to make a row referring to Figure 3. Press seams in one direction.

6. Join the remaining two same-color A-B units to complete a second row, again referring to Figure 3; press seams in one direction.

7. Join the two rows as shown in Figure 4 to complete one Zigzag block; press seams in one direction.

Figure 4

8. Repeat steps 5–7 to complete six blocks in each color combination to total 48 Zigzag blocks.

9. Join six same-color blocks to complete a horizontal row referring to the Placement Diagram; press seams in one direction. Repeat for eight rows.

10. Join the rows referring to the Placement Diagram to complete the pieced top; press seams in one direction.

Completing the Quilt

1. Sandwich the batting between the completed top and prepared backing; pin or baste layers together to hold.

2. Quilt as desired by hand or machine; remove pins or basting. Trim excess backing and batting even with quilt top.

3. Join binding strips on short ends to make one long strip. Fold the strip in half along length with wrong sides together; press.

4. Sew binding to quilt edges, mitering corners and overlapping ends. Fold binding to the back side and stitch in place to finish. ∎

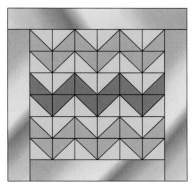

Crooked Paths Table Topper
Placement Diagram
40" x 40"
9 Blocks
3 rows of 3 blocks each

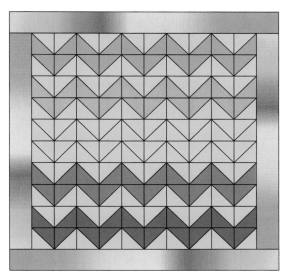

Crooked Paths Throw
Placement Diagram
60" x 60"
25 Blocks
5 rows of 5 blocks each

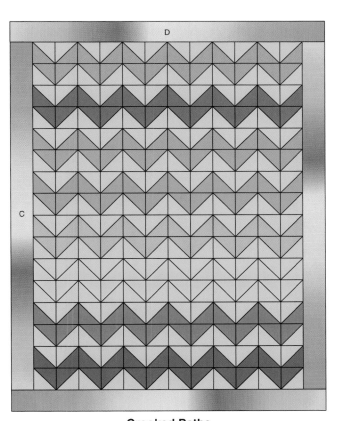

Crooked Paths
Placement Diagram
70" x 90"

Crooked Paths Queen Quilt
Placement Diagram
90" x 90"
64 Blocks
8 rows of 8 blocks each

Crooked Paths Runners

Use a smaller square to make a runner to match the Crooked Paths bed quilt or use totally different color combinations to make fun runners for other areas of your home.

PROJECT SPECIFICATIONS

Skill Level: Beginner
Runner Size: 36" x 18"
Block Size: 6" x 6"
Number of Blocks: 10 for each runner

FABRIC & BATTING FOR RUNNER A

- $1/8$ yard each 5 different bright prints
- $1/4$ yard background fabric
- $1/2$ yard border and binding fabric
- Backing 40" x 22"
- Batting 40" x 22"

FABRIC & BATTING FOR RUNNER B

- $1/4$ yard bright print
- $1/4$ yard background fabric
- $1/4$ yard border and binding fabric
- Backing 40" x 22"
- Batting 40" x 22"

SUPPLIES & TOOLS FOR BOTH

- Neutral color all-purpose thread
- Quilting thread
- Basic sewing tools and supplies

RUNNER A

Cutting

1. Cut two $3^7/8$" by fabric width strips background fabric; subcut strips into (20) $3^7/8$" A squares.

Zigzag A
6" x 6" Block

2. Cut four $3^7/8$" x $3^7/8$" squares from each of the five bright prints.

3. Cut two $3^1/2$" x $30^1/2$" C strips and two $3^1/2$" x $18^1/2$" D strips border fabric.

4. Cut three $2^1/4$" by fabric width strips binding fabric.

Completing the Zigzag A Blocks

1. Draw a diagonal line from corner to corner on the wrong side of each A square.

2. Layer an A square with a B square with right sides together.

3. Stitch $1/4$" on each side of the marked line on the layered units as shown in Figure 1.

Figure 1

4. Cut apart on the marked line and press B open to complete two A-B units as shown in Figure 2; repeat for eight units of each color combination.

Figure 2

5. Select four same-color A-B units; join two units to make a row referring to Figure 3. Press seams in one direction.

Figure 3

6. Join the remaining two same-color A-B units to complete a second row, again referring to Figure 3; press seams in one direction.

7. Join the two rows as shown in Figure 4 to complete one Zigzag A block; press seams in one direction.

Figure 4

8. Repeat steps 5–7 to complete two blocks in each of the five color combinations to total 10 Zigzag A blocks.

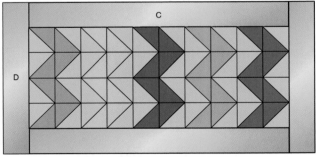

Crooked Paths Table Runner A
Placement Diagram
36" x 18"

Completing the Runner A Top

1. Join two same-color Zigzag A blocks to complete a vertical row referring to the Placement Diagram; press seams in one direction. Repeat for five rows.

2. Join the rows referring to the Placement Diagram to complete the pieced top; press seams in one direction.

3. Sew a C strip to opposite long sides and D strips to the short ends to complete the pieced runner A top; press seams toward C and D strips.

Completing Runner A

1. Sandwich the batting between the completed top and prepared backing; pin or baste layers together to hold.

2. Quilt as desired by hand or machine; remove pins or basting. Trim excess backing and batting even with runner top.

3. Join binding strips on short ends to make one long strip. Fold the strip in half along length with wrong sides together; press.

4. Sew binding to runner edges, mitering corners and overlapping ends. Fold binding to the back side and stitch in place to finish.

RUNNER B

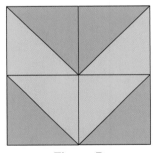

Zigzag B
6" x 6" Block

Cutting

1. Cut two 3⁷⁄₈" by fabric width strips each background fabric (A) and bright print (B); subcut strips into (20) each 3⁷⁄₈" A and B squares.

2. Cut two 3¹⁄₂" x 30¹⁄₂" C strips and two 3¹⁄₂" x 18¹⁄₂" D strips border fabric.

3. Cut three 2¹⁄₄" by fabric width strips binding fabric.

Completing the Zigzag B Blocks

1. Complete 10 Zigzag B blocks referring to the block drawing and Completing the Zigzag A Blocks steps 1–7.

Completing Runner B Top

1. Join five Zigzag B blocks to complete a horizontal row referring to the Placement Diagram; press seams in one direction. Repeat for a second row; press seams in the opposite direction from the previously stitched row.

2. Join the rows referring to the Placement Diagram for positioning.

3. Sew a C strip to opposite long sides and D strips to the short ends to complete the pieced runner B top; press seams toward C and D strips.

Completing Runner B

1. Refer to Completing Runner A to complete runner B. ■

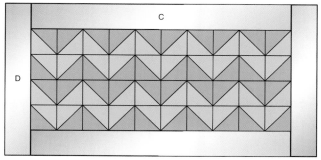

Crooked Paths Table Runner B
Placement Diagram
36" x 18"

Pineapple Fields

Stitch squares at the corners on the diagonal to create the triangle corners of these large Pineapple blocks.

PROJECT NOTES

There are many ways to sew a Pineapple block. Most involve a lot of measuring and cutting exact pieces with angles. This is not a lot of fun as far as I am concerned.

Using squares for the corner triangles may use more fabric, but it speeds up the sewing process, something I am always ready to do. It is also quite accurate.

And, there's a bonus pattern (see page 35) in this book that will use up most of the leftover triangles that were cut off.

Vary the number of blocks per row and the number of rows to create different-size projects as shown with the accompanying drawings.

PROJECT SPECIFICATIONS

Skill Level: Intermediate
Quilt Size: 60" x 60"
Block Size: 30" x 30"
Number of Blocks: 4

FABRIC & BATTING

- 5 yards total assorted bright prints
- Backing 66" x 66"
- Batting 66" x 66"

SUPPLIES & TOOLS FOR BOTH

- Neutral color all-purpose thread
- Quilting thread
- Basic sewing tools and supplies

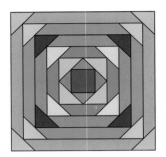

Pineapple
30" x 30" Block

Cutting

1. Cut four $5^1/_2$" x $5^1/_2$" assorted bright print A squares.

2. For one block, cut two 3" x $5^1/_2$" B strips and two 3" x $10^1/_2$" C strips from one bright print.

3. Cut two 3" x $10^1/_2$" D strips and two 3" x $15^1/_2$" E strips from one bright print.

4. Cut two 3" x $15^1/_2$" F strips and two 3" x $20^1/_2$" G strips from one bright print.

5. Cut two 3" x $20^1/_2$" H strips and two 3" x $25^1/_2$" I strips from one bright print.

6. Cut two 3" x $25^1/_2$" J strips and two $30^1/_2$" K strips from one bright print.

7. Repeat steps 2–6 to cut pieces for three more blocks.

8. Cut 20 sets of four matching L squares $5^1/_2$" x $5^1/_2$" from bright prints.

9. Cut $2^1/_4$"-wide strips from bright prints to total 275" for binding.

Completing the Blocks

1. To complete one Pineapple block, sew B to the top and bottom of an A square; press seams toward B.

2. Repeat with two C strips on the remaining sides of A to complete the block center as shown in Figure 1.

Figure 1

3. Draw a diagonal line from corner to corner on the wrong side of four matching L squares.

4. Place an L square right sides together on one corner of the block center as shown in Figure 2; stitch on the marked line. Press L to the right side.

Figure 2

5. Fold L back and trim the extra L layer ¼" from the seam line, leaving the block center intact as shown in Figure 3. Set aside trimmed triangle for the bonus project.

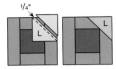

Figure 3

6. Repeat step 5 on each corner of the block center to complete a center unit. ***Note:*** *If the L triangles extend beyond the B and C strips, trim even with B and C. If the strips extend beyond the edges of L, do not trim these even with L.*

7. Continue adding strips and L squares around the center unit in alphabetical order until there are five strips on each side of A to complete one Pineapple block as shown in Figure 4. Repeat for four Pineapple blocks.

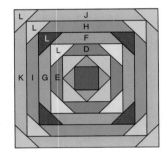

Figure 4

Completing the Top

1. Join two Pineapple blocks to make a row; repeat for two rows. Press seam in rows in opposite directions.

2. Join the rows to complete the pieced top; press seam in one direction.

Completing the Quilt

1. Sandwich the batting between the completed top and prepared backing; pin or baste layers together to hold.

2. Quilt as desired by hand or machine; remove pins or basting. Trim excess backing and batting even with quilt top.

3. Join binding strips on short ends with diagonal seams to make one long strip as shown in Figure 5. Fold the strip in half along length with wrong sides together; press.

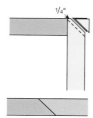

Figure 5

4. Sew binding to quilt edges, mitering corners and overlapping ends. Fold binding to the back side and stitch in place to finish. ■

Pineapple Fields
Placement Diagram
60" x 60"

Pineapple Fields Twin Quilt
Placement Diagram
60" x 90"
6 Blocks

Pineapple Fields Queen Quilt
Placement Diagram
90" x 90"
9 Blocks

Pineapple Place Mats

Stitch squares on the corners of each round of strips to make these quick-to-stitch place mats.

PROJECT NOTES

The list of materials includes enough fabric to make two place mats.

PROJECT SPECIFICATIONS

Skill Level: Beginner
Project Size: 18" x 12"

FABRIC & BATTING

- Bright prints as follows:
  2 ($3^1/_2$" x $9^1/_2$") A
  8 (2" x 2") B
  4 (2" x $9^1/_2$") C
  4 (2" x $6^1/_2$") D
  8 ($3^1/_2$" x $3^1/_2$") E
  4 (2" x $12^1/_2$") F
  4 (2" x $9^1/_2$") G
  8 ($3^1/_2$" x $3^1/_2$") H
  4 (2" x $15^1/_2$") I
  4 (2" x $12^1/_2$") J
  8 ($3^1/_2$" x $3^1/_2$") K
- $1/_3$ yard lime green print for binding
- 2 (22" x 16") rectangles backing
- 2 (22" x 16") rectangles batting

SUPPLIES & TOOLS

- Neutral color all-purpose thread
- Quilting thread
- Basic sewing tools and supplies

Cutting

1. Cut four $2^1/_4$" by fabric width strips lime green print for binding.

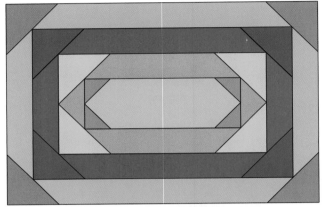

Pineapple Place Mat
Placement Diagram
18" x 12"

Completing the Place-Mat Tops

1. To complete one place-mat top, mark a diagonal line from corner to corner on the wrong side of each B, E, H and K square.

2. Referring to Figure 1, pin and stitch a B square to opposite corners of A; press B to the right side.

Figure 1

3. Fold B pieces back and trim the extra B layer $1/_4$" from the seam line, leaving the A piece intact as shown in Figure 2. Repeat on remaining corners of A to complete an A-B unit as shown in Figure 3.

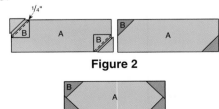

Figure 2

Figure 3

4. Sew C pieces to opposite long sides and D pieces to the short ends of the A-B unit as shown in Figure 4; press seams toward C and D pieces.

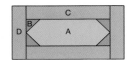

Figure 4

5. Repeat steps 2 and 3 with E squares as shown in Figure 5.

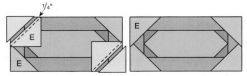

Figure 5

6. Repeat steps 2–4 with F and G strips and H squares and I and J strips and K squares as shown in Figure 6 to complete one place-mat top. Repeat for two tops.

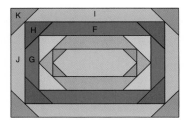

Figure 6

Completing the Place Mats

1. Sandwich one batting rectangle between one completed place-mat top and one prepared backing piece; pin or baste layers together to hold. Repeat with the second place-mat top, batting and backing pieces.

2. Quilt each layered unit as desired by hand or machine; remove pins or basting. Trim excess backing and batting even with place-mat tops.

3. Join binding strips on short ends to make one long strip. Fold the strip in half along length with wrong sides together; press.

4. Sew binding to place-mat edges, mitering corners and overlapping ends. Fold binding to the back sides and stitch in place to finish. ▪

Something for Nothing

Use up the triangles trimmed off the units stitched for Pineapple Fields to make Something for Nothing.

PROJECT SPECIFICATIONS
Skill Level: Beginner
Quilt Size: 21" x 21"

FABRIC & BATTING
- 36 each light and dark triangles set aside from the large Pineapple Fields (page 28), or 18 each light and dark 5½" x 5½" squares bright prints
- ¼ yard binding fabric
- Backing 25" x 25"
- Batting 25" x 25"

SUPPLIES & TOOLS
- Neutral color all-purpose thread
- Quilting thread
- Template plastic
- Basic sewing tools and supplies and 6" acrylic square

Instructions
1. Prepare a triangle template using pattern given.

2. Arrange the leftover triangles into one pile of dark and one of light.

3. Place the triangle template on the wrong side of each light triangle; trace along the diagonal line of the template onto the fabric as shown in Figure 1.

Figure 1

4. Pair each marked light triangle with a dark triangle, aligning corners.

5. Stitch on the marked line; press seam to the dark triangle.

6. Repeat for 36 stitched units.

7. Divide the stitched units evenly into two piles; label them A and B.

8. Draw a diagonal line from one corner to another across the previously stitched seam on the wrong side of each A unit as shown in Figure 2.

Figure 2   **Figure 3**   **Figure 4**

9. Match one A unit with one B unit right sides together with the light fabric in the A unit on top of the dark fabric in the B unit as shown in Figure 3.

10. Stitch ¼" on each side of the marked line on the A unit as shown in Figure 4.

11. Cut apart on the drawn line to make two A-B units as shown in Figure 5; press units open.

Figure 5

12. Using the acrylic square, trim each A-B unit to 4" x 4" as shown in Figure 6.

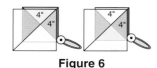

Figure 6

13. Repeat for 36 A-B units.

14. Join the A-B units in pairs as shown in Figure 7; press seams toward darker fabrics.

Figure 7

15. Join three A-B pairs to make a row as shown in Figure 8; repeat for six rows. Press seams in one direction.

Figure 8

16. Join the rows, referring to the Placement Diagram for positioning of strips; press seams in one direction.

17. Cut three 2¹⁄₄" by fabric width strips binding fabric.

18. Sandwich the batting between the completed top and prepared backing; pin or baste layers together to hold.

Triangle Template

19. Quilt as desired by hand or machine; remove pins or basting. Trim excess backing and batting even with quilt top.

20. Join binding strips on short ends to make one long strip. Fold the strip in half along length with wrong sides together; press.

21. Sew binding to quilt edges, mitering corners and overlapping ends. Fold binding to the back side and stitch in place to finish.

Making Quilt Without Leftover Triangles

1. Draw a diagonal line from corner to corner on the light 5¹⁄₂" x 5¹⁄₂" squares.

2. Match a light square with a dark square with right sides together; sew ¹⁄₄" on each side of the drawn line referring to Figure 9.

Figure 9

3. Cut apart on drawn line and press seams to the darker fabric.

4. Continue stitching as in step 6 of the Instructions to complete the quilt. ■

Something for Nothing
Placement Diagram
21" x 21"

Confused Stars

Different-size points appear on opposite sides of the star-within-stars design.

PROJECT NOTES

Wider borders may be added to the completed top to make a crib-size quilt. Four completed Confused Stars tops stitched in two rows of two tops each finish as a queen-size quilt.

PROJECT SPECIFICATIONS

Skill Level: Beginner
Quilt Size: $39^1/_2$" x $44^1/_2$"

FABRIC & BATTING

- $^1/_4$ yard pink print
- $^1/_2$ yard yellow print
- $^7/_8$ yard orange print
- 1 yard green print
- 1 yard multicolor print
- Backing 46" x 51"
- Batting 46" x 51"

SUPPLIES & TOOLS FOR BOTH

- Neutral color all-purpose thread
- Quilting thread
- Basic sewing tools and supplies

Cutting

1. Cut one $6^1/_2$" x $10^3/_4$" A rectangle and four each $2^1/_2$" x $2^1/_2$" B and $3^1/_2$" x $3^1/_2$" C squares pink print.

2. Cut one each $3^1/_2$" x $10^3/_4$" D, $2^1/_2$" x $10^3/_4$" E, $3^1/_2$" x $6^1/_2$" F and $2^1/_2$" x $6^1/_2$" J rectangles and two $2^1/_2$" x $3^1/_2$" G rectangles yellow print.

3. Cut five $3^1/_2$" x $3^1/_2$" H squares and one $2^1/_2$" x $2^1/_2$" I square yellow print.

4. Cut one each 6" x $15^3/_4$" L, 6" x $11^1/_2$" M, $3^1/_2$" x $15^3/_4$" N and $3^1/_2$" x $11^1/_2$" R rectangles and two $3^1/_2$" x 6" P rectangles orange print.

5. Cut five 6" x 6" O, one $3^1/_2$" x $3^1/_2$" Q and four $8^3/_4$" x $8^3/_4$" S squares orange print.

6. Cut one each $8^3/_4$" x $24^1/_4$" T, $8^3/_4$" x 20" U, 6" x $24^1/_4$" and 6" x 20" Z rectangles and two 6" x $8^3/_4$" X rectangles green print.

7. Cut one each $8^3/_4$" x $8^3/_4$" W and 6" x 6" Y squares green print.

8. Cut one strip each of the following from multicolor print: 3" x 38" AA, $4^1/_4$" x 38" BB, $3^1/_4$" x 40" CC and $4^3/_4$" x 40" DD.

9. Cut five $2^1/_4$" by fabric width strips multicolor print.

Completing the Top

1. Draw a diagonal line from corner to corner on the wrong side of each B, C, K and S square and four each H and O squares.

2. Referring to Figure 1, pin and stitch a B square on each end of J; trim the extra B layer $1/_4$" from the seam line, leaving the J layer in place. **Note:** *Trimming only the excess B layer reduces bulk and adds stability. You may trim both B and J layers to a $1/_4$" seam, if desired.*

Figure 1

3. Repeat step 2 with B on each end of E and C on each end of F and D to complete pieced units as shown in Figure 2.

Figure 2

4. Sew a B-J unit to the top and a C-F unit to the bottom of A as shown in Figure 3; press seams toward A.

Figure 3

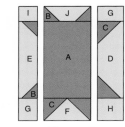

Figure 4

5. Sew I and G to the ends of the B-E unit and G and H to the ends of the C-D unit as shown in Figure 4; press seams away from B-E and C-D. Sew these pieced units to opposite sides of A, again referring to Figure 4 to complete the center unit; press seams toward A.

6. Repeat step 2 to make K-M, H-N, K-L and H-R units as shown in Figure 5.

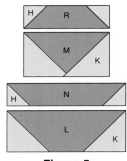

Figure 5

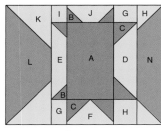

Figure 6

7. Sew the K-L and H-N units to opposite long sides of the center unit as shown in Figure 6; press seams away from the center unit.

8. Sew O and P to opposite ends of the K-M unit to complete an O-K-M-P unit as shown in Figure 7; press seams toward O and P.

Figure 7

9. Sew Q and P to opposite ends of the H-R unit to complete a P-H-R-Q unit as shown in Figure 8; press seams toward P and Q.

Figure 8

10. Sew the O-K-M-P unit to the top and the P-H-R-Q unit to the bottom of the center unit as shown in Figure 9; press seams away from the center unit.

11. Repeat step 2 to make O-Z, O-V, S-U and S-T units referring to Figure 10.

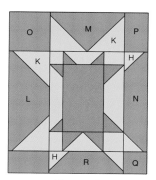

Figure 9

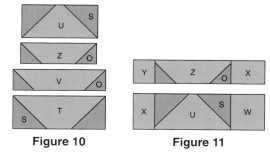

Figure 10   **Figure 11**

12. Sew X and Y to the ends of the O-Z unit and X and W to the ends of the S-U unit as shown in Figure 11; press seams toward X and Y and X and W.

13. Sew the O-V and S-T units to opposite long sides of the center unit as shown in Figure 12; press seams away from the center unit.

14. Sew the X-O-Z-Y unit to the top and the X-S-U-W unit to the bottom of the center unit, again referring to Figure 12; press seams away from the center unit.

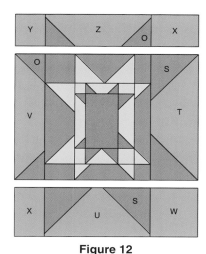

Figure 12

Confused Stars
Placement Diagram
39½" x 44½"

15. Sew the AA strip to the V edge and the BB strip to the T edge of the pieced center; press seams toward AA and BB strips.

16. Sew the CC strip to the top and the DD strip to the bottom of the pieced center to complete the pieced top; press seams toward CC and DD strips.

Completing the Quilt

1. Sandwich the batting between the completed top and prepared backing; pin or baste layers together to hold.

2. Quilt as desired by hand or machine; remove pins or basting. Trim excess backing and batting even with quilt top.

3. Join binding strips on short ends to make one long strip. Fold the strip in half along length with wrong sides together; press.

4. Sew binding to quilt edges, mitering corners and overlapping ends. Fold binding to the back side and stitch in place to finish. ∎

Wacky Stars Table Topper

Pieced stars shine against a pale background in this pretty table topper.

PROJECT SPECIFICATIONS

Skill Level: Intermediate
Quilt Size: 34" x 34"
Block Size: 9" x 9"
Number of Blocks: 9

FABRIC & BATTING

- $^1/_8$ yard each 9 bright prints
- $^1/_4$ yard purple tonal
- $^3/_4$ yard multicolor bright print
- $^7/_8$ yard light blue tonal
- Backing 40" x 40"
- Batting 40" x 40"

SUPPLIES & TOOLS FOR BOTH

- Neutral color all-purpose thread
- Quilting thread
- Basic sewing tools and supplies

Cutting

1. Cut one $3^1/_2$" x $3^1/_2$" A square from each bright print.

2. Cut four $2^1/_2$" by fabric width strips light blue tonal; subcut strips into nine $2^1/_2$" B squares, (18) $3^1/_2$" E rectangles and (17) $4^1/_2$" D rectangles.

3. Cut three $4^1/_2$" by fabric width strip light blue tonal; subcut strips into nine $4^1/_2$" C squares, (18) $3^1/_2$" G rectangles and one $2^1/_2$" x $4^1/_2$" D rectangle.

4. Make 18 copies each of the E/F and G/H foundation units using patterns given.

5. Cut two each $2^1/_2$" x 3" F and $2^1/_8$" x $5^3/_4$" H rectangles from each bright print.

6. Cut two $1^1/_2$" x $27^1/_2$" I strips and two $1^1/_2$" x $29^1/_2$" J strips purple tonal.

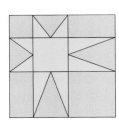

Uneven Star
9" x 9" Block

7. Cut two 3" x $29^1/_2$" K strips and two 3" x $34^1/_2$" L strips multicolor bright print.

8. Cut four $2^1/_4$" by fabric width strips multicolor bright print for binding.

Completing the Blocks

1. Cut each F rectangle in half from corner to corner to make F and FR triangles as shown in Figure 1. Repeat with H rectangles to make H and HR.

| **Figure 1** | **Figure 2** | **Figure 3** |

2. Pin an E rectangle to the unprinted side of an E/F foundation unit; pin an F triangle right sides together with the E piece on the 1-2 edge, allowing fabric to extend at least $^1/_4$" as shown in Figure 2; pin along the 1-2 line. Fold F over to cover area 2 as shown in Figure 3. Adjust fabric if necessary. Unfold fabric F to lie flat on E.

3. Flip paper pattern; stitch on the 1-2 line, stitching from outside edge to outside edge of pattern as shown in Figure 4.

4. Trim the 1-2 seam allowance to $1/8"-1/4"$ as shown in Figure 5. Fold F to the right side; lightly press with a warm dry iron.

Figure 4

Figure 5

5. Repeat steps 2–4 with FR; trim excess on edges even with cutting line as shown in Figure 6. Repeat for all E-F and G-H units.

6. To complete one block, select same-fabric E-F and G-H units. Sew a G-H unit to one side and an E-F unit to the opposite side of A to complete the center row as shown in Figure 7; press seams toward A.

Figure 6

Figure 7

7. Sew B and D to the F ends of the remaining E-F unit; press seams toward B and D. Sew to the top of the center row, again referring to Figure 7; press seams toward the center row.

8. Sew C and D to the H sides of the remaining G-H unit; press seams toward C and D. Sew to the bottom of the center row to complete one block, again referring to Figure 7; press seams toward the center row. Repeat for nine Uneven Star blocks.

Completing the Top

1. Arrange three blocks to make a row referring to the Placement Diagram for positioning of blocks; repeat for three rows. Join blocks in rows; press seams in alternate rows in opposite direction. Join rows to complete the pieced center; press seams in one direction.

2. Sew the I strips to opposite sides and J strips to the top and bottom of the pieced center; press seams toward I and J strips.

3. Sew the K strips to opposite sides and L strips to the top and bottom of the pieced center; press seams toward K and L strips to complete the top.

Completing the Quilt

1. Sandwich the batting between the completed top and prepared backing; pin or baste layers together to hold.

2. Quilt as desired by hand or machine; remove pins or basting. Trim excess backing and batting even with quilt top.

3. Join binding strips on short ends to make one long strip. Fold the strip in half along length with wrong sides together; press.

4. Sew binding to quilt edges, mitering corners and overlapping ends. Fold binding to the back side and stitch in place to finish. ■

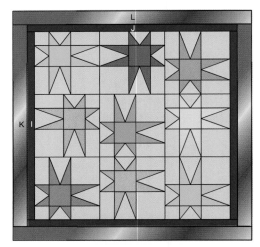

Wacky Stars Table Topper
Placement Diagram
34" x 34"

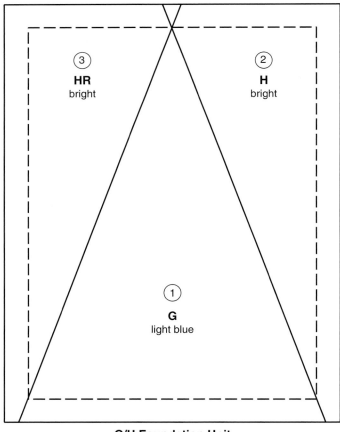

G/H Foundation Unit
Make 18 copies

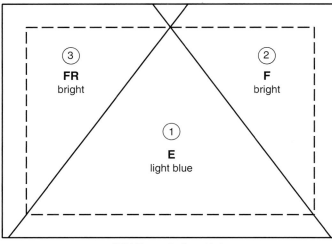

E/F Foundation Unit
Make 18 copies

Wacky Stars Place Mats

Make a set of two place mats to match the Wacky Stars Table Topper.

PROJECT SPECIFICATIONS

Skill Level: Intermediate
Project Size: 18" x 12"
Block Size: 6" x 6"
Number of Blocks: 4 (for 2 place mats)

FABRIC & BATTING

- $1/8$ yard each 2 bright prints
- $7/8$ yard blue print
- 2 (22" x 16") rectangles backing
- 2 (22" x 16") rectangles batting

SUPPLIES & TOOLS

- Neutral color all-purpose thread
- Quilting thread
- Basic sewing tools and supplies

Cutting

1. Cut the following from each bright print: two $2^3/4$" x $2^3/4$" A squares, eight 2" x $2^1/2$" E rectangles and eight $1^3/4$" x $3^5/8$" F rectangles.

2. Cut the following from blue print: four 2" x 2" B squares, (12) $2^3/4$" x $2^3/4$" C squares and (16) 2" x $2^3/4$" D rectangles.

3. Cut two $12^1/2$" x $12^1/2$" G squares blue print.

4. Make eight copies each of the D/E and C/F foundation units using patterns given.

5. Cut four $2^1/4$" by fabric width strips blue print for binding.

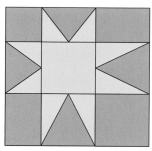

Uneven Star
6" x 6" Block

Completing the Blocks

1. Cut each E rectangle in half from corner to corner to make E and ER triangles as shown in Figure 1. Repeat with F rectangles to make F and FR.

Figure 1   **Figure 2**

2. Pin a D rectangle to the unprinted side of a D/E foundation unit; pin an E triangle right sides together with the D piece on the 1-2 edge as shown in Figure 2; pin along the 1-2 line. Fold E over to cover area 2, allowing fabric to extend at least $1/4$" as shown in Figure 3. Adjust fabric if necessary. Unfold fabric E to lie flat on D.

Figure 3   **Figure 4**

3. Flip paper pattern; stitch on the 1-2 line, stitching from outside edge of pattern to outside edge of pattern as shown in Figure 4.

4. Trim the 1-2 seam allowance to $1/8$"–$1/4$" as shown in Figure 5. Fold E to the right side; lightly press with a warm dry iron.

Figure 5

Figure 6

5. Repeat steps 2–4 with ER; trim excess on edges even with cutting line as shown in Figure 6. Repeat for all D-E and C-F units.

6. To complete one block, select same-fabric D-E and C-F units. Sew a C-F unit to one side and a D-E unit to the opposite side of A to complete the center row as shown in Figure 7; press seams toward A.

Figure 7

HOUSE OF WHITE BIRCHES, BERNE, INDIANA 46711   WWW.WHITEBIRCHES.COM

7. Sew B and D to the E ends of the remaining D-E unit; press seams toward B and D. Sew to the top of the center row, again referring to Figure 7; press seams toward the center row.

8. Sew C and D to the F sides of the remaining C-F unit; press seams toward C and D. Sew to the bottom of the center row to complete one block, again referring to Figure 7; press seams toward the center row. Repeat for four blocks.

Completing the Top

1. To complete one place-mat top, join two different-color blocks as shown in Figure 8; press seams in one direction.

Figure 8

2. Sew the G square to the left-side edge of the joined-blocks section referring to the Placement Diagram; press seams toward G to complete one place-mat top. Repeat for two place-mat tops.

Completing the Place Mats

1. Sandwich one batting rectangle between one completed place-mat top and one prepared

backing piece; pin or baste layers together to hold. Repeat with the second place-mat top and batting and backing pieces.

2. Quilt each layered unit as desired by hand or machine; remove pins or basting. Trim excess backing and batting even with place-mat top.

3. Join binding strips on short ends to make one long strip. Fold the strip in half along length with wrong sides together; press.

4. Sew binding to place-mat edges, mitering corners and overlapping ends. Fold binding to the back sides and stitch in place to finish. ■

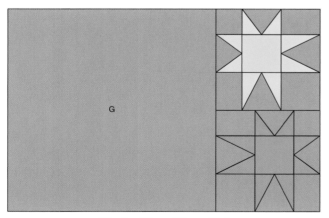

Wacky Stars Place Mat
Placement Diagram
18" x 12"

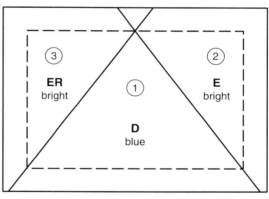

D/E Foundation Unit
Make 8 copies

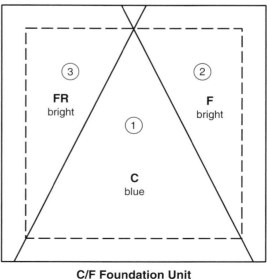

C/F Foundation Unit
Make 8 copies

Garden Maze

Triangles create a maze starting in the center of this colorful quilt.

PROJECT SPECIFICATIONS
Skill Level: Beginner
Quilt Size: $59\frac{1}{2}$" x $59\frac{1}{2}$"

FABRIC & BATTING
- $1\frac{1}{4}$ yards pink mottled
- $1\frac{5}{8}$ yards blue/green batik
- $1\frac{3}{4}$ yards purple mottled
- Backing 65" x 65"
- Batting 65" x 65"

SUPPLIES & TOOLS
- Neutral color all-purpose thread
- Quilting thread
- Basic sewing tools and supplies

Cutting
1. Cut seven $5\frac{7}{8}$" by fabric width strips each pink mottled (A) and blue/green batik (B); subcut strips into (45) $5\frac{7}{8}$" squares each A and B.

2. Cut two $5\frac{1}{2}$" by fabric width strips blue/green batik; subcut strips into (11) $5\frac{1}{2}$" C squares.

3. Cut two $5\frac{1}{4}$" x $50\frac{1}{2}$" D strips and two $5\frac{1}{4}$" x 60" E strips along the length of the purple mottled.

4. Cut five $2\frac{1}{4}$"-wide strips along the remaining length of the purple mottled for binding.

Completing the Units
1. Draw a diagonal line from corner to corner on the wrong side of each A square.

2. Layer an A square with a B square with right sides together.

3. Stitch $\frac{1}{4}$" on each side of the marked line on the layered units as shown in Figure 1.

Figure 1

4. Cut apart on the marked line and press B open to complete two A-B units as shown in Figure 2; repeat for 90 units. Discard one unit.

Figure 2

Completing the Top
1. Arrange the A-B units with the C squares in 10 rows of 10 A-B and C combinations referring to Figure 3.

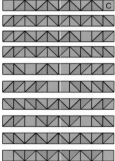

Figure 3

2. Join the units and squares in rows as arranged; press seams in each row in one direction, pressing to opposite sides from row to row to offset seams.

3. Join the rows as arranged to complete the pieced center; press seams in one direction.

4. Sew a D strip to opposite sides and E strips

to the top and bottom of the pieced center to complete the pieced top; press seams toward D and E strips.

Completing the Quilt

1. Sandwich the batting between the completed top and prepared backing; pin or baste layers together to hold.

2. Quilt as desired by hand or machine; remove pins or basting. Trim excess backing and batting even with quilt top.

3. Join binding strips on short ends to make one long strip. Fold the strip in half along length with wrong sides together; press.

4. Sew binding to quilt edges, mitering corners and overlapping ends. Fold binding to the back side and stitch in place to finish. ■

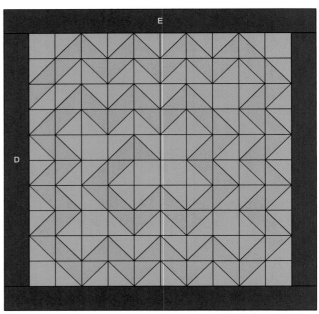

Garden Maze
Placement Diagram
59½" x 59½"

Sunflower Dreams

Appliqué sunflower motifs to a base of pieced strippy scrap blocks to make this whimsical wall quilt.

PROJECT SPECIFICATIONS

Skill Level: Beginner
Quilt Size: 18" x 24"
Block Size: 3" x 3"
Number of Blocks: 48

FABRIC & BATTING

- Assorted bright scraps for dragonfly body and wings
- 5 (2" x 2") scraps for sunflower centers
- 1/4 yard total yellow scraps for sunflower petals
- 3/8 yard total assorted bright green fabrics for blocks and binding
- 1/2 yard total green scraps for stems and leaves
- 1 1/4 yards total assorted blue fabrics for blocks and binding
- Backing 22" x 28"
- Batting 22" x 28"

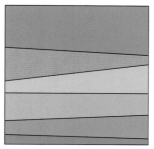

Green Strippy
3" x 3" Block
Make 6

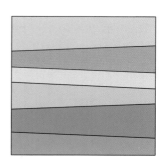

Blue/Green Strippy
3" x 3" Block
Make 3

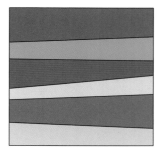

Blue Strippy
3" x 3" Block
Make 39

SUPPLIES & TOOLS

- Neutral color all-purpose thread
- Quilting thread
- 1 1/4 yards 18"-wide fusible web
- Wavy blade with rotary cutter
- 8 (8 1/2" x 11") sheets white paper
- 6" or 6 1/2" acrylic square
- Basic sewing tools and supplies

Cutting

1. Cut 1 1/4"-wide strips from blue fabrics and cut into 5" lengths. You will need 241 blue strips.

2. Cut 1 1/4"-wide strips from assorted bright green fabrics and cut into 5" lengths. You will need 47 green strips.

3. Prepare templates for appliqué shapes using patterns given.

4. Trace shapes onto the paper side of the fusible web as directed on each piece for number to cut.

5. Cut out shapes, leaving a margin around each one.

6. Fuse shapes to the wrong side of fabrics as directed on each piece for color.

7. Cut out the petals on traced lines. Cut leaves and flower centers using the wavy blade on your rotary cutter; remove paper backing.

8. Cut two each 1 1/4" x 19", 1 1/4" x 22" and 1 1/4" x 6" strips fusible web.

9. Cut 1¹/₂"-wide stem pieces from the fusible web as follows: 15¹/₂" A, 12" B, 17" C, 15¹/₂" D and 11" E.

10. Draw a curved stem about ³/₄" wide on each 1¹/₂"-wide strip; fuse strips to the wrong sides of the green scraps.

11. Using the wavy blade on your rotary cutter, cut strips along drawn lines to create stems.

12. Cut (48) 3¹/₂" x 3¹/₂" squares from the 8¹/₂" x 11" white paper.

Completing the Blocks

1. To complete one Green Strippy block, select six different 1¹/₄" x 5" green strips; pin one strip to a paper square on an angle, extending edges of strip off the edges and corners of the paper as shown in Figure 1.

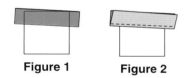

Figure 1   **Figure 2**

2. Place the second strip right sides together with the first strip and stitch with a ¹/₄" seam as shown in Figure 2.

3. Press the stitched strip to the right side.

4. Place a third strip right sides together at an angle with the second strip as shown in Figure 3; stitch as in step 2.

Figure 3   **Figure 4**

5. Trim excess second strip and press the third strip to the right side as shown in Figure 4.

6. Repeat with three more strips until the entire paper is covered as shown in Figure 5.

7. Place stitched block right side down on a rotary-cutting mat; trim fabric edges even with paper edges along the right and bottom edges as shown in Figure 6.

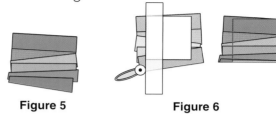

Figure 5   **Figure 6**

8. Carefully remove paper backing, tearing from the edges that have not been trimmed.

9. Using the acrylic square, trim the stitched unit to 3¹/₂" x 3¹/₂" to complete one Green Strippy block as shown in Figure 7. Repeat for six Green Strippy blocks.

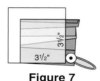

Figure 7

10. Repeat all steps with assorted 1¹/₄" x 5" blue strips to complete 39 Blue Strippy blocks.

11. Repeat all steps to make two Blue/Green Strippy blocks with two blue and four green strips and one with three each blue and green strips.

Completing the Top

1. Select six Blue Strippy blocks; join to make a row referring to Figure 8; press seams in one direction. Repeat for six rows; press seams in adjacent rows in opposite direction. Join the rows referring to the Placement Diagram for positioning; press seams in one direction.

Figure 8   **Figure 9**

2. Join three Blue Strippy blocks with three Blue/Green Strippy blocks to make a row as shown in Figure 9; press seams in one direction. Sew to the bottom of the previously stitched blue-row section; press seam in one direction.

3. Join the six Green Strippy blocks to make a row referring to Figure 10; press seams in one direction. Sew to the bottom of the previously stitched row to complete the pieced section of the top.

Figure 10

4. Referring to Figure 11, arrange the stem pieces on the pieced section; when satisfied with placement, fuse in place.

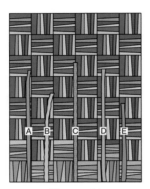

Figure 11

5. Arrange 12 petals and one flower center at the top of each stem, overlapping petals as necessary. When satisfied with positioning, fuse in place.

6. Arrange leaves on stalks referring to the Placement Diagram for positioning; fuse in place.

7. Place the dragonfly bodies and wings above the flowers referring to the Placement Diagram for positioning; when satisfied with placement, fuse in place.

Completing the Quilt

1. Sandwich the batting between the completed top and prepared backing piece.

2. Set up your sewing machine with a darning foot. Lower the feed dogs. Using thread to match appliqués in the top and thread to match backing in the bobbin, machine-stitch close to the edges of each appliquéd piece.

3. Meander-quilt in the background areas using thread to match fabrics.

4. Fuse one 19" and both 22" fusible-web strips to the wrong side of blue fabrics; fuse the remaining fusible-web strips to the wrong side of green fabrics.

5. Cut along one long edge of each strip using the wavy blade on your rotary cutter; cut remaining edges even with strip edges.

6. Fold the wavy edge of one strip over to meet the straight edge with the paper inside; crease. Repeat with all strips.

7. Remove paper backing from one 22" blue strip. Align crease with one side edge of the quilted piece with the wavy edge on the front side, extending the end of the strip 1/4" into the green on the Blue/Green Strippy block. Trim strip even with quilt at top edge.

8. Very carefully fuse front edge of strip to the front side of the quilted piece; do not touch the back half of the strip with the iron.

9. Fold strip over to the back side of the quilted piece; pull tight and fuse in place.

10. Repeat with one 6" green strip at the bottom of same side edge, overlapping blue strip to match binding color to block color.

11. Repeat steps 7–10 on remaining side edge.

12. Fold the 19" blue strip in half along length; cut one end at a 45-degree angle. Measure against the top of the quilted piece; mark opposite end and cut strip at a 45-degree angle as shown in Figure 12.

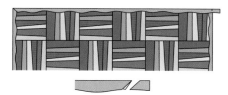

Figure 12

13. Fuse this strip to the quilt top as for side binding strips.

14. Repeat steps 12 and 13 for green strip at bottom edge.

15. Machine-stitch several curvy quilting lines through the binding as in step 2 to complete the quilt. ■

Sunflower Dreams
Placement Diagram
18" x 24"

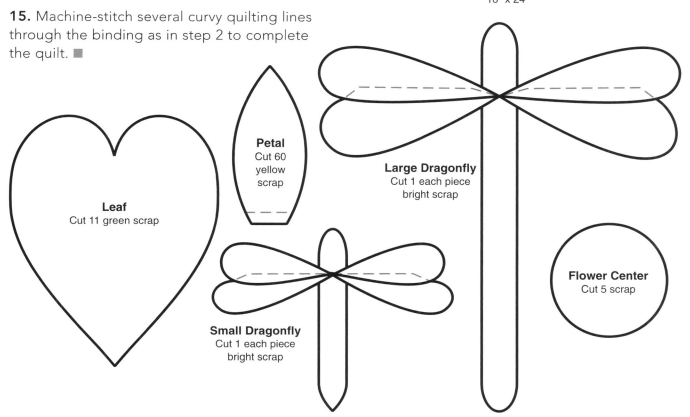

Leaf
Cut 11 green scrap

Petal
Cut 60
yellow
scrap

Large Dragonfly
Cut 1 each piece
bright scrap

Small Dragonfly
Cut 1 each piece
bright scrap

Flower Center
Cut 5 scrap

Bright & Sassy Purse

You just need two Uneven Log Cabin blocks to create a sassy quilted purse

PROJECT SPECIFICATIONS
Skill Level: Beginner
Project Size: $8^3/_4$" x 11"
Block Size: $8^3/_4$" x 11"
Number of Blocks: 2

FABRIC & BATTING
- $1/_2$–$3/_4$ yard total bright prints
- Lining $9^1/_4$" x $22^1/_4$"
- Batting $3^1/_2$" x $9^1/_4$" and $9^1/_4$" x $22^1/_4$"

SUPPLIES & TOOLS
- Neutral color all-purpose thread
- Quilting thread
- 6" of $1/_2$"-wide hook-and-loop tape
- Basic sewing tools and supplies

Cutting
1. Cut one strip each 3" x 18" and 3" x 42" from one bright print for straps.

2. Cut two $1^3/_4$" x 4" A pieces bright prints.

3. Cut a variety of $1^1/_4$" strips bright prints for block rounds; subcut strips into two pieces in each of the following sizes: #1–$1^3/_4$", #2–$4^3/_4$", #3–$2^1/_2$", #4–$5^1/_2$", #5–$3^1/_4$", #6–$6^1/_4$", #7–4", #8–7", #9–$4^3/_4$", #10–$7^3/_4$", #11–$5^1/_2$", #12–$8^1/_2$", #13–$6^1/_4$", #14–$9^1/_4$", #15–7", #16–10", #17–$7^3/_4$", #18–$10^3/_4$", #19–$8^1/_2$", #20–$11^1/_2$" and #21–$9^1/_4$".

4. Cut one $3^1/_2$" x $9^1/_4$" C flap piece bright print and one for lining.

Completing the Blocks
1. Referring to Figure 1, sew pieces around the A center in numerical order, pressing seam away from A after each strip is added, to complete one Uneven Log Cabin block; repeat for two blocks.

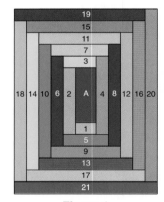

Figure 1

Completing the Purse Top
1. Join two Uneven Log Cabin blocks together on the #21 strip ends as shown in Figure 2 to piece the purse top; press seam open. Set aside.

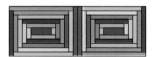

Figure 2

2. Measure and mark $1^1/_4$" in from the bottom left corner and $1^1/_4$" up from the bottom left corner

on the wrong side of the flap lining piece as shown in Figure 3.

Figure 3

3. Draw a line connecting the two marks, again referring to Figure 3.

4. Repeat steps 2 and 3 on the bottom right corner as shown in Figure 4.

Figure 4

5. Place the C flap piece right side up on the 3¹/₄" x 9¹/₄" batting piece with one long edge aligned; pin the flap lining piece right sides together with C, aligning the marked edge with the batting and top aligned edges.

6. Using a ¹/₄" seam allowance, stitch along both short ends and along the bottom edge of the layered flap pieces as shown in Figure 5.

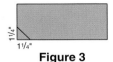

Figure 5

7. Sew along the previously marked lines on the corners as shown in Figure 6; trim corners to ¹/₄", again referring to Figure 6. Trim batting close to the stitching.

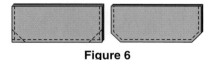

Figure 6

8. Turn stitched flap right side out through opening; press.

9. Topstitch ¹/₄" from stitched edges as shown in Figure 7.

Figure 7   **Figure 8**

10. Center and stitch the loop side of the hook-and-loop tape ¹/₄" from the finished edge of the lining side of the stitched flap as shown in Figure 8.

Completing the Purse

1. Place the stitched purse top on the 9¹/₄" x 22¹/₄" batting rectangle; pin to hold.

2. Baste layers together ¹/₈" from raw edge all around.

3. Stitch in the ditch between seam joining the two blocks as shown in Figure 9. Hand- or machine-quilt remainder of the layered top as desired.

Figure 9

4. Center the flap piece right sides together on one end of the quilted top; baste ¹/₈" from edge of the quilted top as shown in Figure 10.

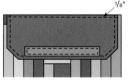 

Figure 10   **Figure 11**

5. Center the hook strip of the hook-and-loop tape 2" down from the remaining short end of the quilted top as shown in Figure 11; stitch in place.

6. Referring to Figure 12, fold the lining fabric with right sides together, matching raw edges; stitch down one side. Stitch remaining side, leaving a 4" opening.

Figure 12

7. Fold the quilted top at the joined seam with right sides together, matching all edges; stitch down both sides. Turn right side out.

8. Slip the quilted top inside the stitched lining piece. **Note:** *The right side of the quilted top should touch the right side of the lining piece.* Pin side seams together with flap between the quilted top and the lining.

9. Stitch ¹/₄" from top raw edge all around though all layers as shown in Figure 13.

Figure 13

10. Turn purse right side out through opening in the lining; hand-stitch lining opening closed. Push lining inside purse.

11. Topstitch ¹/₄" around top edge of purse.

12. Join the 3" x 18" and 3" x 42" fabric strips on the 3" ends to make a long strip for the handle; press seam to one side.

13. Press under ¹/₄" on each long edge of the handle as shown in Figure 14.

Figure 14

14. Fold the pressed strip along length with wrong sides together, matching folded edges as shown in Figure 15; press.

Figure 15

15. Unfold edges at each end of the strip and join ends to make a tube; press seam to one side. Refold pressed edges and stitch close to folded edges as shown in Figure 16 to hold and complete handle.

Figure 16

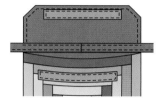

Figure 17

16. Position the handle on the inside of the flap with overlapped portion of handle in the center as shown in Figure 17; stitch in place to complete the purse. ◼

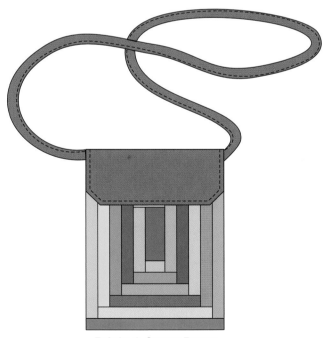

Bright & Sassy Purse
Placement Diagram
8³/₄" x 11"

Grab & Go Bottle Cover

Make a bright-color bottle cover with a small pocket for change to take your cold drink with you anywhere.

PROJECT SPECIFICATIONS
Skill Level: Beginner
Project Size: Fits a 20-ounce bottle

FABRIC & BATTING
- 11" x 9$^1/_4$" rectangle bright print for outside piece
- 11" x 8$^3/_4$" rectangle bright print for lining
- 1" x 2" rectangle bright print for loop
- 3$^1/_2$" x 6$^1/_2$" rectangle bright print for pocket
- 2 (3$^1/_2$" x 2") rectangles bright print for pocket flap
- 10$^1/_2$" x 7$^1/_4$" rectangle cotton batting

SUPPLIES & TOOLS
- Neutral color all-purpose thread
- Quilting thread
- 8$^1/_2$" piece $^1/_4$"-wide elastic
- 8" piece $^1/_4$"-wide ribbon
- 2" of $^1/_2$"-wide hook-and-loop tape
- 1 carabiner key chain
- Basic sewing tools and supplies

Instructions
1. Sandwich and pin the batting rectangle between the outside and lining rectangles with batting $^3/_4$" down from the top and centered side to side on the outside rectangle as shown in Figure 1; set aside.

Figure 1

2. Fold the 3$^1/_2$" x 6$^1/_2$" pocket piece with right sides together and stitch the short ends, leaving a 1" opening in the center of the seam as shown in Figure 2.

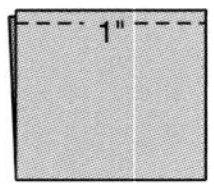

Figure 2

3. Fold the stitched piece with right sides together with the opening centered as shown in Figure 3; stitch a $^1/_4$" seam down each side edge, again referring to Figure 3.

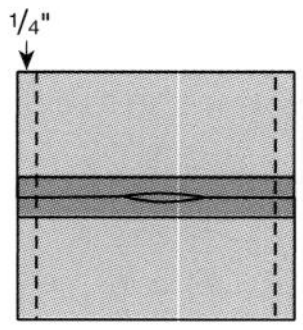

Figure 3

4. Turn stitched piece right side out through the opening; slipstitch the opening closed. Press.

5. Pin the two 3$^1/_2$" x 2" pocket flap rectangles right sides together; sew a $^1/_4$" seam on both short ends and one long edge as shown in Figure 4.

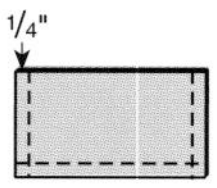

Figure 4

6. Clip corners and turn stitched flap pieces right side out; press flat.

HOUSE OF WHITE BIRCHES, BERNE, INDIANA 46711   WWW.WHITEBIRCHES.COM

7. Center and sew the hook tape to the inside edge of the flap piece and the loop tape to the top edge of the pocket piece as shown in Figure 5.

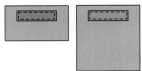

Figure 5

8. Referring to Figure 6, center the pocket piece 2¹/₂" up from bottom edge of the layered bottle cover; topstitch pocket in place around sides and bottom.

2¹/₂"

Figure 6

9. Position the flap piece ¹/₄" above the stitched pocket piece and stitch ¹/₄" from the raw edge as shown in Figure 7. **Note:** *You might want to zigzag-stitch along the raw edge of the flap to prevent raveling.*

¹/₄"

Figure 7

10. Fold the 1" x 2" loop piece in half to make a piece ¹/₂" x 2". Open and fold raw edges in to the fold line and fold again; press. The strip now measures ¹/₄" x 2. Stitch along the long open edge to finish the loop.

11. Fold the loop in half and pin 1³/₄" from the top edge of the layered bottle cover with raw edges of loop aligned with side edge as shown in Figure 8; machine-baste to hold.

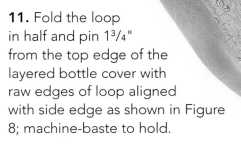

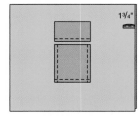

1³/₄"

Figure 8

12. Fold the layered bottle cover right sides together along the long edges and stitch using a ¹/₄" seam allowance.

13. Fold ¹/₂" up from bottom edge to the inside; stitch about ¹/₈" from raw edge, leaving a ¹/₂" opening unstitched.

14. Run the ¼"-wide ribbon through the opening and around the stitched casing; pull up to tighten and knot ends to secure. Trim ends to about 1" long. Tack in place inside bottle cover, making sure stitches do not show on the outside.

15. Fold ½" down from the top edge to the inside; stitch about ⅛" from raw edge, leaving a 1" opening as shown in Figure 9.

½" ↘ ↞1"↠

Figure 9

16. Thread elastic through the opening and out the other end; join the elastic ends. Stitch remainder of casing closed.

17. Turn right side out; attach the carabiner key chain to the loop to finish. ■

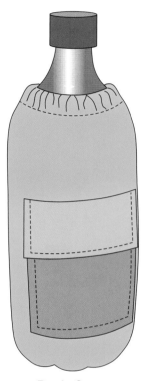

Bottle Cover
Placement Diagram
Fits 20-Ounce Bottle

Changing Size of Bottle Cover to Fit Bottles

You may change the size of the fabric and batting pieces to fit different-size bottles.

1. Measure around the widest part of the bottle; add 2" to this measurement for the size to cut the outside fabric.

2. Measure from the center of the bottom of the bottle up the side of the bottle to the height you want the cover to reach. Add 1¼"

to this measurement. This is the height to cut the outside fabric.

3. Cut the lining the same width and ½" smaller than the height of the outside fabric.

4. Cut the batting ½" smaller than the width and 1½" shorter than the height of the outside fabric.

5. You may make larger pockets for larger bottle covers, if desired.

Metric Conversion Charts

Metric Conversions

U.S. Measurements		Multiplied by		Metric Measurement
yards	x	.9144	=	meters (m)
yards	x	91.44	=	centimeters (cm)
inches	x	2.54	=	centimeters (cm)
inches	x	25.40	=	millimeters (mm)
inches	x	.0254	=	meters (m)

Metric Measurements		Multiplied by		U.S. Measurements
centimeters	x	.3937	=	inches
meters	x	1.0936	=	yards

Standard Equivalents

U.S. Measurement		Metric Measurement		
1/8 inch	=	3.20 mm	=	0.32 cm
1/4 inch	=	6.35 mm	=	0.635 cm
3/8 inch	=	9.50 mm	=	0.95 cm
1/2 inch	=	12.70 mm	=	1.27 cm
5/8 inch	=	15.90 mm	=	1.59 cm
3/4 inch	=	19.10 mm	=	1.91 cm
7/8 inch	=	22.20 mm	=	2.22 cm
1 inch	=	25.40 mm	=	2.54 cm
1/8 yard	=	11.43 cm	=	0.11 m
1/4 yard	=	22.86 cm	=	0.23 m
3/8 yard	=	34.29 cm	=	0.34 m
1/2 yard	=	45.72 cm	=	0.46 m
5/8 yard	=	57.15 cm	=	0.57 m
3/4 yard	=	68.58 cm	=	0.69 m
7/8 yard	=	80.00 cm	=	0.80 m
1 yard	=	91.44 cm	=	0.91 m

Embroidery Stitch Guide

Buttonhole Stitch

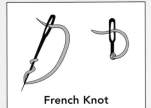

French Knot

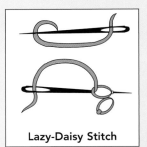

Lazy-Daisy Stitch

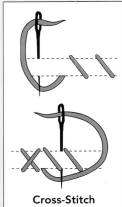

Cross-Stitch

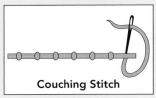

Couching Stitch

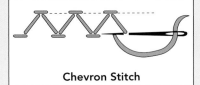

Chevron Stitch

Satin Stitch

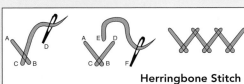

Herringbone Stitch

Stem Stitch

Fly Stitch

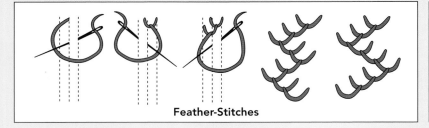

Feather-Stitches

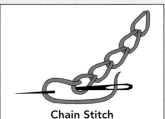

Chain Stitch

E-mail: Customer_Service@whitebirches.com

HOUSE of WHITE BIRCHES
PUBLISHERS SINCE 1947

Hot! Bright Quilting is published by House of White Birches, 306 East Parr Road, Berne, IN 46711, telephone (260) 589-4000. Printed in USA. Copyright © 2006 House of White Birches.

RETAIL STORES: If you would like to carry this pattern book or any other House of White Birches publications, call the Wholesale Department at Annie's Attic to set up a direct account: (903) 636-4303. Also, request a complete listing of publications available from House of White Birches.

Every effort has been made to ensure that the instructions in this pattern book are complete and accurate. We cannot, however, take responsibility for human error, typographical mistakes or variations in individual work.

ISBN: 978-1-59217-106-4
2 3 4 5 6 7 8 9

STAFF
Editors: Jeanne Stauffer, Sandra L. Hatch
Associate Editor: Dianne Schmidt
Technical Artist: Connie Rand
Copy Supervisor: Michelle Beck
Copy Editors: Nicki Lehman, Mary O'Donnell, Judy Weatherford
Graphic Arts Supervisor: Ronda Bechinski

Graphic Artist: Nicole Gage
Art Director: Brad Snow
Assistant Art Director: Nick Pierce
Photography: Tammy Christian, Don Clark, Matthew Owen, Jackie Schaffel
Photo Stylists: Tammy Nussbaum, Tammy M. Smith